Bloom

Adult Coloring Book

Belongs to:

_____

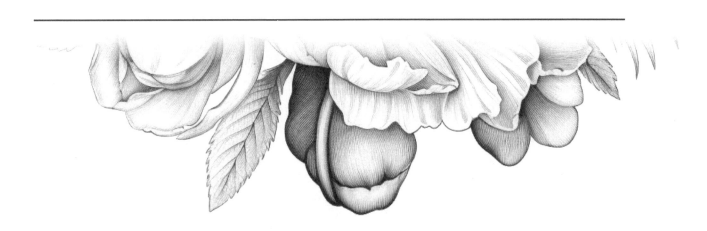

A Message From The Author

We hope that you love this book
and enjoy every single page.
If you like this book please
give us your honest feedback
on amazon.
It's really helpful for us.

Made in United States
Troutdale, OR
03/11/2024

18361304R00060